STRENGTHENING DEMOCRATIC LOCAL GOVERNANCE (SDLG) PROGRAM IN BANGLADESH

WORK PLAN 2014-15

CONTENTS

ACRONYMS AND ABBREVIATIONS

ACT	Actions Combatting Trafficking in Persons
CiG	Citizens-in-Governance Forum
CREL	Climate Resilient Environments and Livelihoods
COR	Contract Officer's Representative
LG	Local Government
LGCI	Local Government Capacity Index
LGU	Local Government Unit
NHSDP	NGO Health Service Delivery Project
M&E	Monitoring and Evaluation
MLGRD	Ministry of Local Government, Rural Development and Cooperatives
MP	Members of Parliament
NGO	Nongovernmental Organization
PHR	Protecting Human Rights
SDLG	Strengthening Democratic Local Governance Program
UP	Union Parishad
USAID	United States Agency for International Development

1.0 INTRODUCTION

The Strengthening Democratic Local Governance in Bangladesh (SDLG) Project as extended is a 51-month activity (December 2010–March 2015) funded by the United States Agency for International Development's Bangladesh Mission (USAID/Bangladesh). Building on more than a decade's worth of local government strengthening programs in Bangladesh, the SDLG Project combines a focus on research and policy advocacy, capacity development for local government associations, and training and technical assistance for local government units at union parishad, upazila parishad (UP), and pourashava levels. Tetra Tech ARD is the implementing partner for the SDLG Project.

Key elements of the SDLG Project strategy for achieving results include:

- Building on USAID/Bangladesh's more than 10-year history of significant local governance support programs.

- Enhancing the political will of national and local government elected officials as well as citizen groups and NGOs to reform local governance.

- Identifying and disseminating to local governments innovative practices to achieve performance standards.

- Integrating gender and youth concerns across the SDLG program, while supporting women's participation in local government leadership.

- Disseminating through multiple media outlets information on local governments in Bangladesh and the role of the USAID-funded SDLG Project.

- Linking with USAID/Bangladesh's (and other donor's) programs, including Presidential Initiatives in the areas of health, agriculture and climate change.

This strategic approach will help ensure the project achieves core objectives within the 51-month timeframe, given the resources available, and taking into consideration constraints and opportunities posed by the legal and policy framework for local governments.

1.1 COLLABORATION WITH USAID SECTOR PROJECTS

Focus on Health, Agriculture, Human Rights and Climate Change in Extension Year

In 2013, SDLG implemented activities to strengthen local government standing committee (SC) oversight of service delivery with women representatives in key leadership roles. This set of activities was supported with Windows of Opportunity funds after review and consent of the USAID COR. In 2014, SDLG will draw on this experience with local committees overseeing health, agricultural and human rights services, and on its work mobilizing communities through Citizens in Governance (CiG) forums, to link USAID sector project activities to local government structures to improve their effectiveness and sustainability.

Collaboration activities with different USAID projects in health, agriculture, human rights and also climate change are designed to support sector goals while strengthening the union and upazila systems that monitor the quality of central government service delivery. Activities will be conducted in a limited set of SDLG target local government units (LGUs) that overlap with different sector project sites.

2.0 COMPONENTS AND TASK AREAS

In this section, we present a work plan for the SDLG extension period of March 31, 2014 – March 29, 2015. Our discussion is organized according to the three component areas identified by USAID/Bangladesh in the Statement of Work (SOW) provided in the modification to contract dated February 26, 2014. For clarity, we further divide activities under Component Two into two tasks: Improve LGU Management Performance; and Enhance LGU—Sector Collaboration for Service Delivery. We similarly divide activities under Component Three into two tasks: Improve Citizen Participation in Local Governance; and Improve Citizen Oversight of LGUs and Sector Service Delivery. We also present the anticipated timing for activities and refer to the expected "program deliverables" that were noted in the SOW (Section VI), when relevant.

2.1 COMPONENT 1 – ROLES AND AUTHORITIES OF LOCAL GOVERNMENTS

2.1.1 APPROACH TO COMPONENT 1

In the 2011-2013 period, SDLG conducted primary research and mounted public and private advocacy events to increase policy maker understanding of the potential for improved local revenues and services under the new local government acts, as well as the need for 'fine tuning' of these acts with specific policy reforms. LGA leaders participated in SDLG preparatory sessions to assist them in articulating well-researched and rational demands for policy reforms. At the union and paurashava levels, the reforms identified were improvements to an otherwise sound set of rules and regulations.

However, at the upazila level, reform is badly needed before these councils can effectively exercise authority to improve service delivery. The inability of upazilas to ensure cooperation of service providers in improving services provided by health and family planning workers, primary school teachers, agricultural extension officers, human rights officers, and others remains an obstacle to increasing service quality. However, the reform needed for this to occur is little recognized and how upazilas and unions would coordinate under the law to improve services is little understood. Activities under this component will focus on advancing upazila policy reform while showcasing how the upazila and union systems can function to improve health, agriculture, human rights and climate change adaptation.

ACTIVITY 1: NATIONAL CONFERENCES ON LG POLICY AND PRACTICE

Approach: During the extension period, SDLG will organize two national conferences focused on local governance policy and practice issues. Target participants include the LG Parliamentary Standing Committee, LG Division, UzPAB, civil society, donor partners and media representatives. We will also advance conference themes through select meetings with Ministry of Local Government (MLGRD) policy makers, including continuing joint and additional secretaries with whom SDLG developed relations during its 2011-2013 period of performance. Conference themes are as follows:

National Conference on Upazila Policy and Practice: The upazila system was only recently re-activated following elections in 2009. Ambiguities in the law and statutory regulations, and the absence of established practices have generated much confusion, some conflicts and mixed performance at this level of local government. The objective of this conference is to 'model' the functioning of a upazila in practice to (a) demonstrate that upazila parishads can function under existing law and policies, (b) detail the role of information flows from union to upazila standing committees to improve services, and (c) highlight again the importance of a key upazila policy reform to support upazila effectiveness in improving sector service delivery. This policy reform was identified by grantee US and SDLG in 2013 and was the subject of 2013 advocacy but is still awaiting GoB Cabinet approval. Model upazila research featured in the conference will include examples of benefits to health, agriculture, human rights and climate change adaptation that result from the functioning of a model upazila.

- *Program Deliverable -- Research Product:* Findings of research supporting this national conference will be produced and disseminated to key stakeholders in booklets tentatively entitled 'Working Together to Improve Services: A Model of Practice for Unions, Upazilas and Line Ministry Officials' featuring examples of upazila-level action to improve sector services. This research will draw on field testing of the union – upazila interaction developed in previous SDLG research and incorporated into 2012-2013 union and upazila trainings.

National Conference on 'Best Practices' in Local Service Delivery: This conference will focus on how union and paurashava level oversight can improve service delivery to citizens. Consistent with SDLG's methodology of working through and seeking to improve existing LGU systems, the conference will focus on standing committees, and how citizens and LGU officials can work with and through SCs to improve services. The conference will highlight examples from SDLG field work under Components 2 and 3 of benefits to health, agriculture, human rights and climate change adaptation that result from effectively functioning standing committees.

- *Program Deliverable -- Research Product:* Findings of research supporting this national conference will be produced and disseminated to key stakeholders in booklets tentatively entitled 'Standing Committees, Citizens and Best Practice for Improved Local Service Delivery'. The booklet will feature examples from sector collaboration from SDLG 2014 field activities. This research will draw on field testing of the standing committee oversight role recommended in previous SDLG research and incorporated into 2012-13 union and paurashava trainings.

Timing: National Conference on Upazila Policy and Practice, Q2 2014; National Conference on 'Best Practices' in Local Service Delivery, Q3 2014.

2.2 COMPONENT 2 – TRANSPARENT AND EFFECTIVE SERVICE DELIVERY BY LOCAL GOVERNMENTS

2.2.1 APPROACH TO COMPONENT 2

Project activities from 2011-2013 have equipped local councils and communities with a functioning set of governance practices based on law that promote accountability and transparency. These practices have produced measurable results with increased local revenues, greater citizen participation (including through the SDLG-supported CiG groups) and improved services. SDLG plans to deepen and expand these practices with an emphasis on standing committee oversight to increase their utility to USAID sector project service improvement goals while continuing to support past successful practices as needed. To do so, it will employ many of the same approaches and activities that contributed to previous project results.

In addition, as part of the focus on sector service delivery, SDLG will work with related upazila councils and upazila SCs to strengthen partnerships among and with these LGUs as needed if service issues cannot be resolved at the union or paurashava levels.

FOUNDATIONAL ACTIVITY 1: ORGANIZE PLANNING MEETINGS WITH TARGET LGUS AND CIGS WITH SECTOR PARTICIPATION

Approach: The purpose of these one-day, non-residential planning meetings will be to liaise with stakeholders from LGUs, CIGs, sectors and implementing partners to discuss the SDLG extension work plan and calendar. This meeting will introduce the sector participants and implementing partners to the SDLG methodology for working with LGUs.

This activity also serves as a foundational activity for our approach to Component 3 as noted below.

Timing: Q1 2014.

FOUNDATIONAL ACTIVITY 2: ESTABLISH EXTENSION PERIOD TECHNICAL APPROACH WITH PARTNER NGOS (PNGOS) AND USAID SECTOR PROJECT PARTNERS

Approach: The SDLG implementation methodology includes working with and through PNGOs in the delivery of training and technical assistance to LGUs and local communities. For the extension period, our PNGOs will provide refresher trainings to LGUs and CiGs based on modified versions of previously developed core training curricula as well as provide newly developed trainings focused on monitoring and reporting on service delivery for Standing Committees.

Under this activity we will take the following steps with our PNGOs, as well as USAID sector project field staff working to promote health, agriculture, human rights and climate change project objectives:

- **Program Orientation:** This will be a four-hour non-residential session for SDLG leaders and technical staff to brief relevant PNGO officers on SDLG's overall technical approach during the extension period. USAID sector project representatives will also introduce their activities and discuss areas of collaboration with SDLG.

- **Refresher Training for PNGOs:** This will be a one-day residential training to review with PNGOs the core training curricula for LGUs and CiGs previously developed, and to discuss methods for tailoring the curricula in order to address distinct management performance deficits in different LGUs. Collaborative activities identified with USAID sector projects will also be reviewed.

- **Training for PNGOs on Monitoring and Reporting for Standing Committees:** This will be a three-day, train-the-trainer session in which SDLG leaders and technical staff present newly-developed training materials to PNGOs and coach them in how to present the material to LGUs and CIGs. The new training material will focus on monitoring and reporting on service delivery for Standing Committees as well as on collaborative activities in health, agriculture, human rights and climate change.

This activity also serves as a foundational activity for our approach to Component 3 as noted below.

Timing: All steps to be completed in Q1 2014.

2.2.2 TASK 1 – IMPROVE LGU MANAGEMENT PERFORMANCE

ACTIVITY 1: STRENGTHEN LGU MANAGEMENT PERFORMANCE THROUGH TARGETED REFRESHER TRAININGS

Approach: SDLG developed three core training modules which were delivered to 600 UPs, paurashavas and upazilas during 2012-2013. In the extension period, we will provide two-day residential refresher trainings for the smaller number of extension period-targeted union and municipal councils. The refresher trainings will be customized to focus on known performance deficits in the target LGUs. In this, SDLG previously adopted an "ABC" scoring system to grade overall progress of the LGUs in applying lessons from the initial trainings. In partnership with SDLG PNGOs, we will tailor trainings in the extension period to the LGU's ABC score card, and focus in particular on functional governance processes requiring support. Within the targeted number of LGUs, there will be approximately 10 UPs which did not originally receive the SDLG core trainings. For these LGUs, we will provide an intensive version of the original training program.

Timing: Q2 2014.

ACTIVITY 2: DEMAND-DRIVEN FACILITATION AND MENTORING FOR LGUS

Approach: SDLG understands that LGUs cannot be expected to immediately and effectively practice all of the expert guidance we provide simply by participating in core trainings. Rather, the learning and adoption of new practices is iterative, and so our methodology includes plans for our own senior technical staff as well as our PNGOs to facilitate and mentor LGUs over time as they reform practices and improve management performance. Such assistance ranges from providing guidance on the phone, informal meetings with key LGU or community members, reviewing required documentation of LGU activities, and observing and providing feedback to LGUs as they conduct their business. Based on our experience during 2012-2013, such facilitation and mentoring is often most helpful when it is demand-driven as this indicates the desire of LGUs and CIGs to improve their performance. We anticipate providing facilitation and mentoring in this fashion again for a variety of local governance processes, such as ward planning and open budget meetings, tax assessment and collection, financial record keeping and five-year development planning. Where appropriate, SDLG will support USAID sector project field staff to integrate outreach to citizens and councils during these local governance processes.

Timing: Q2 – Q4 2014.

ACTIVITY 3: PEER LEARNING FOR NEW LGUS

Approach: For the small number of new unions that have not received SDLG training in core governance practices from 2012-2013, we will additionally use 'peer learning' techniques to supplement the Activities 1 and 2 above. Our approach will involve identifying experienced councilors and CiG members who will join in SDLG training sessions in new unions. These councilors and citizens will share their experiences, including references to specific reforms that were adopted by their unions and overviews of the impacts that resulted.

Timing: Q2 – Q3 2014

2.2.3 TASK 2 – ENHANCE LGU – SECTOR COLLABORATION FOR SERVICE DELIVERY

ACTIVITY 1: IMPROVE LGU SERVICE DELIVERY THROUGH TRAININGS FOR SECTOR STANDING COMMITTEES

Approach: Standing Committees are an important means through which LGUs can improve service delivery, and through which service delivery performance may be monitored and reported on in a systematic and transparent manner. During 2012-2013, SDLG supported various SCs to develop monitoring tools with checklists of central government services mandated for the locality. These tools enabled committees to perform site visits and to monitor and subsequently report back on actual service delivery performance. In 2014, these tools will incorporate additional questions provided by USAID sector partners in support of their project objectives.

During the extension period, we will provide two-day, non-residential dedicated trainings for certain sector-specific SCs to ensure committee members fully understand their responsibilities and authorities, and have the tools to effectively monitor and report. SDLG will focus on working with four key sector SCs in UPs and paurashavas, and with related upazila sector SCs on an as-needed basis. The four SCs are Agriculture; Health and Family Planning; Women and Children Welfare; and Audit and Accounts. In many cases we will involve USAID sector project field staff in health, agriculture, human rights and/or climate change in these trainings to allow them to present their work and its relevance to service delivery to SC members, and to establish follow-on linkages with the SCs when appropriate.

Program Deliverable – Standardized Action Plans. In conjunction with these trainings, we will work with sector-specific SCs to develop and adopt actions plans for monitoring and improving service delivery. These plans will build on the methodology SDLG developed during 2012-2013 for SC service monitoring checklists as mentioned above.

Timing: Q2 – Q3 2014.

ACTIVITY 2: DEMAND-DRIVEN FACILITATION AND MENTORING FOR STANDING COMMITTEES

Approach: As discussed above, the SDLG implementation methodology involves informal follow-up with program beneficiaries to help them implement reforms and practices taught in our core training curricula. We anticipate providing facilitation and mentoring in this manner, often demand-driven, for a variety of sector SCs. This may involve collaboration with USAID sector projects and SCs when they have identified areas of common interest and ways they may usefully work together toward the common goal of improved service delivery.

Program Deliverable – Improved Service Delivery. The SDLG approach of working with and through Standing Committees, and ensuring mobilized citizens participate in the SCs as mandated by law, will lead to better LGU and citizen monitoring and oversight of service delivery. When combined with our geographic focus and efforts to link with other USAID and donor programs, SDLG anticipates supporting a number of cases (minimum of 10) where SCs and public officials directly work to improve service delivery in the areas of health, food security, climate change and/or other USAID priority areas.

Timing: Q2 – Q4 2014.

2.3 COMPONENT 3 – CITIZEN PARTICIPATION IN LOCAL DECISION-MAKING

2.3.1 APPROACH TO COMPONENT 3

Activities under this Component work in parallel with those outlined under Component 2. As in the 2012-2013 period, active participation by informed citizens with their local governments, especially with Standing Committees, will be key to activating the local governance structures that guide revenue generation, planning and budgeting, and service delivery. Our approach will ensure that citizens are both trained together with council members as well as provided separate, sector-specific training and technical assistance for their roles as members of Standing Committee. In the extension period, we will apply many of the same proven approaches with citizens that contributed to earlier project results.

FOUNDATIONAL ACTIVITY 1: ORGANIZE PLANNING MEETING WITH TARGET LGUS AND CIGS WITH SECTOR PARTICIPATION

This activity serves as a foundation for both Component 2 and Component 3. It was discussed above under the Task 1, Activity 1 of Component 2.

FOUNDATIONAL ACTIVITY 2: ESTABLISH EXTENSION PERIOD TECHNICAL APPROACH WITH PARTNER NGOS

This activity serves as a foundation for both Component 2 and Component 3. It was discussed above under the Task 1, Activity 2 of Component 2.

ACTIVITY 1: CITIZENS-IN-GOVERNANCE GROUPS REFRESHER TRAINING

Approach: SDLG provided technical assistance to assist councils in forming CiG groups in 500 UPs during 2012-2013, and provided core training for them on the three governance themes. In the extension period, we will provide a one-day, non-residential refresher training for CIGs in the target UPs. In partnership with the SDLG PNGOs, we will assess knowledge gaps to identify areas for CiG groups improvement, and tailor the trainings accordingly. Where appropriate, SDLG will support USAID sector partner field staff to engage with CiGs to support their citizen outreach and mobilization goals.

As many CiG members participate on UP Standing Committees, they will also benefit from the two-day, non-residential trainings provided for SCs as described under Task 2, Activity 1 under Component 2.

Timing: Q1 2014.

2.3.3 TASK 2 – INCREASE CITIZEN OVERSIGHT OF LGUS AND SECTOR SERVICE DELIVERY

ACTIVITY 1: COMMUNITY DRAMA WITH FOCUS ON STANDING COMMITTEES AND SECTOR ISSUES

Approach: In 2013, SDLG supported partner NGOs to organize folk dramas performed at local community levels. The script for the dramas was developed collaboratively with NGOs and SDLG's lead communications agency partner integrating logos and themes from the larger SDLG communications campaign and IEC materials. Our innovative methodology involved having LGU officials, CiG group participants and other community members be the actors and perform the drama after receiving expert training from PNGO drama troupes. Through the plot of the dramas, and the active participation of LGU officials, this activity helped teach community members about local government processes under the law and the important role of citizen participation in good governance.

For the extension period, we will adopt this methodology to again organize folk dramas at the community level. The plot and focus of the dramas will incorporate health, agriculture, human rights and climate change issues facing the community, and will examine ways that citizens can work with local authorities as well as sector projects to ensure needed services are provided.

Timing: Q3 – Q4 2014.

ACTIVITY 2: CITIZEN 'EYE REPORTING' BY LOCAL YOUTH VIA SOCIAL MEDIA

Approach: As part of its wide-ranging communications program, SDLG in 2011-2013 explored the potential for youth in promoting good governance and social change via digital and social media. After an initial workshop in 2012 for 24 youths, an expanded group of 48 youth from SDLG intervention sites were provided customized training in 2013. These youth learned how local governance can meet local needs, how to create video 'Eye Reports' on local issues, and how to share these reports using digital and social media platforms. A group of 15 to 20 finalists with the best video documentaries participated in a 3-day workshop in January 2014 conducted by an international specialist in social media.

In the extension period, SDLG will work with these finalists to carry forward their learning, supporting them in engaging and teaching other potential youth video journalists in neighboring areas to develop and publish video 'Eye Reports' via social media. Many of these new aspiring video journalists will be based in SDLG's 2014 intervention areas and will be encouraged to include the role of Standing Committees in improving sector services in their videos.

Timing: Q2 – Q3 2014.

3.0 CROSS-CUTTING THEMES AND APPROACHES

3.1 LINKING SDLG TO USAID'S SECTOR PROGRAMS

An important objective during the extension period will be to identify and build linkages between the activities and goals of the SDLG project and the activities and goals of other USAID/Bangladesh projects also present in the target geographic areas (see the following section on our geographic focus). Preliminary discussions conducted by SDLG for this extension period determined the desirability for SDLG to build linkages with mission programs related to the President's Global Health and Feed the Future and Global Climate Change Initiatives as well as with other programs under the portfolio of the Democracy and Governance sector team.

For example, SDLG expects to link with projects such as:
- Engender Health Mayer Hashi II (MH-II) Project;
- Pathfinder International NGO Health Service Delivery Project (NHSDP);
- Dhaka Ahasania Mission (DAM) Agricultural Extension Project;
- Winrock International Climate Resilient Environments and Livelihoods (CREL) Project;
- Plan International Protecting Human Rights (PHR) Project; and
- Winrock International Actions for Combating Trafficking in Persons (ACT) Project.

Broadly speaking, the objective of building linkages will be for SDLG to assist LGUs and local communities to better focus on, respond to and manage important service delivery and local development issues that have also been identified by other USAID projects. In doing so, SDLG will assist in building local ownership and actions (and potentially modest contributions of local resources) that will help improve sector services and, broadly, support locally-identified development priorities. In terms of USAID/Bangladesh's 2011-2016 Results Framework, this approach may contribute to several IRs associated with both the DO2: Food Security Improved and DO3: Health Status Improved. For example, SDLG interventions may support the IR2.1: Sustainably Increased Agricultural Productivity or the IR3.3: Strengthened Health Systems and Governance, among others.

An important means for accomplishing this will be through SDLG's work with Standing Committees, and bringing these SCs better into contact and coordination with community-based groups focused on local issues, whether this be in the areas of health, agriculture, women's rights, family planning or others. On the one hand, SDLG will systematically help council members on SCs understand the responsibilities of local governments on service delivery, and better integrate monitoring and reporting of service delivery performance into the work of local governments. On the other hand, SDLG will work with USAID projects, their local partners and mobilized community groups so that they understand, can advocate to and participate with SCs as an important way to build local ownership and encourage improved services.

3.2   GEOGRAPHIC FOCUS

After preliminary contact with several of the USAID projects noted above, SDLG obtained geographic location lists of sufficient detail to cross-reference with SDLG's existing program intervention sites. A detailed review subsequently identified over 230 overlapping sites with nearby NHSDP health clinics and over 50 shared sites where the DAM Agricultural Extension Project seeks to form farmer producer groups and improve extension services. This review also identified several districts where SDLG sites coincide with either Mayer Hashi, PHR or ACT projects. While the geographic overlap offers abundant opportunities for SDLG-trained local council structures to be engaged in improving sector services, resources available for 2014 will limit the geographic scope of SDLG activities.

Subject to further consultations with the SDLG COR and USAID projects above, we have preliminarily identified 200 sites for advance planning purposes. These include:

- 175 NHSDP Smiling Sun sites including 10 sites for urban health activities;

- 67 sites for possible collaboration with Mayer Hashi II on family planning;

- 48 Ag Extension project sites; and

- Several CREL, PHR and ACT sites

To better understand the challenges in working with non-SDLG trained councils to promote local engagement with sector project work, SDLG has also chosen a small number of new unions to work in outside of its 2011 to 2013 activity area. A map displaying these 200 sites and the sector overlap is provided as **Annex 1**.

3.3   GENDER AND YOUTH

Throughout implementation of all activities, the SDLG Project is reinforcing the capacities of women elected officials and citizens actively participating in their communities to better accomplish their mandates, serve as role models and ensure their contributions to strengthening local governments. In its citizen group activities, the inclusion of youth is emphasized.

SDLG plans for the promotion of gender equity and inclusion of youth in project components include:

Citizen in Governance (CiG) Forums Formation: In 2014, women will continue to represent no less than a third (33%) of the membership of CiG forums. CiG formation process allows for a membership that broadly reflects the gender, economic, social, ethnic and political mix of the local community. The percentage of youth aged 25 and younger in CiGs in 2012-13 was 12%.

Local Government Unit (LGU) Training: By law, each union or municipal council must have at least three women representatives elected to reserved seats. All SDLG LGU trainings include the full council with these women members attending. In 2014, SDLG activities will continue to facilitate a leadership role for women (both local council members and CiG citizen members) many of whom are chairs of the local standing committees that are key channels of citizen input into service delivery.

Monitoring and Evaluation (M&E): In project training activities, the project's M&E system ensures that data is collected and disaggregated by gender.

4.0 MONITORING AND EVALUATION

The Performance Monitoring Plan for the extension period will focus on the calendar year 2014. It will combine quarterly reporting on a targeted set of PMP indicators described below with a modified Local Government Capacity Index (LGCI) as well as an baseline and endline survey and focus groups on knowledge, attitude and practices (KAP) of elected leaders and citizens in intervention and control areas.

PMP Indicators: A revised set of indicators incorporating both governance indicators and sector specific indicators in health, agriculture and climate change provided by the USAID Health and Economic Growth Offices will be submitted following this Work Plan as directed by the USAID COR.

The targeted set of PMP indicators for the extension period will rely on streamlined data collection by partner NGOs with monitoring and quality control by SDLG regional offices and Dhaka office field team leaders. Progress on PMP indicators will be included each quarter as part of the SDLG quarterly reporting to USAID, both in aggregate as well as segregated by gender and by urban and rural location.

LGCI, Endline Survey and Focus Groups: SDLG will conduct a modified **Local Government Capacity Index (LGCI)** focusing on local revenue generation, citizen participation and new measures of service delivery improvement to be developed from performance data collection activities in the intervention areas. The LGCI is one of several "Program Deliverables" identified by USAID/Bangladesh in the SDLG extension SOW. It will provide a picture of improved LGU capacity in services linked to Standing Committee activation as compared to the start of the extension period.

Additionally, we will conduct baseline and endline **Knowledge, Attitude and Practice (KAP) Surveys** as well as supporting **focus groups** with elected representatives and CiG members. The Endline Survey is also one of several "Program Deliverables" identified in the SDLG extension SOW. The survey and focus groups will be used to obtain both quantitative and qualitative information on changes in knowledge, perceptions, and practices of LGUs and citizens in the areas of health, agriculture, human rights, and climate change especially as associated with central government workers or donor-funded NGO activities.

ANNEX 1:

PROJECT EXTENSION YEAR 4 LGU MAPPING

STRENGTHENING DEMOCRATIC LOCAL GOVERNANCE (SDLG)

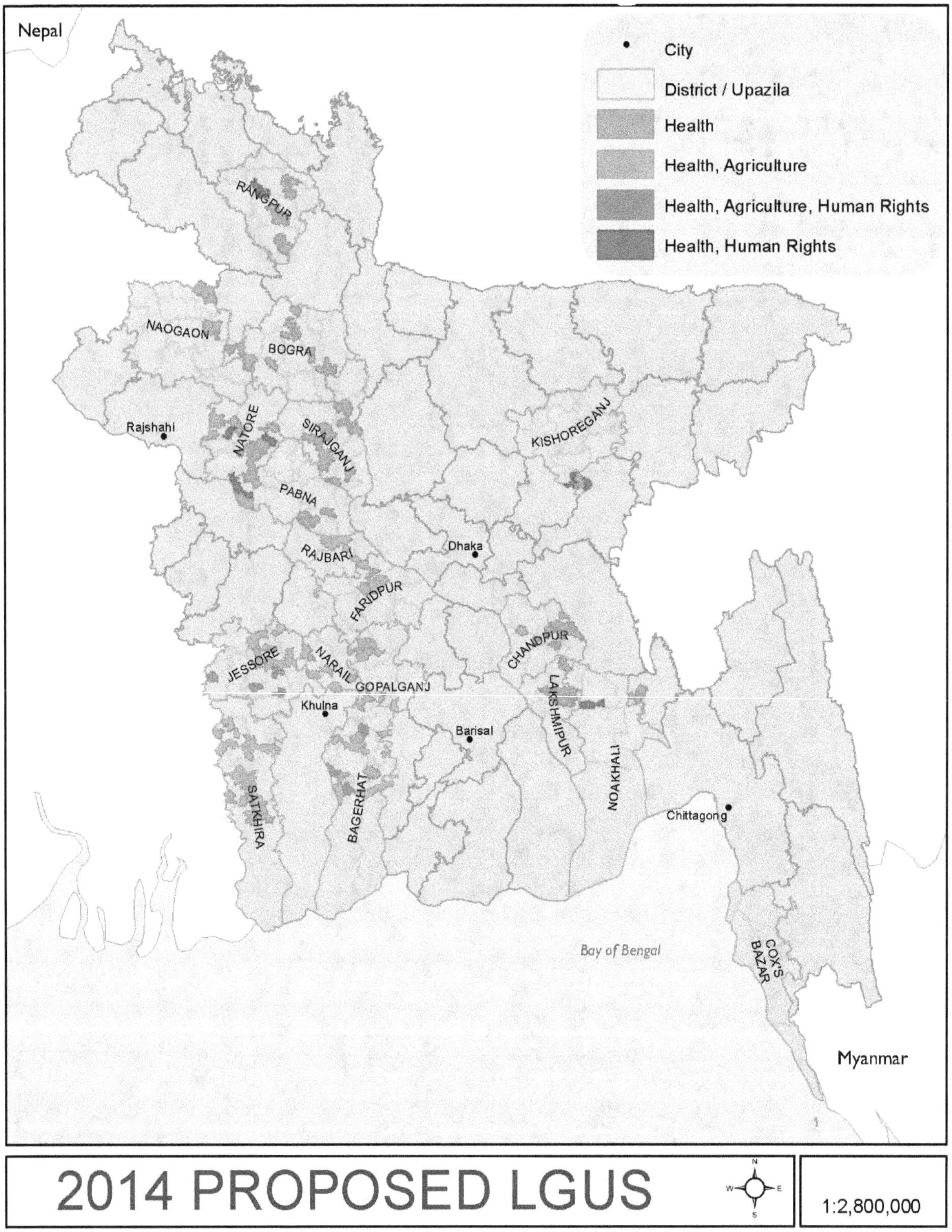
Nepal
City
District / Upazila
Health
Health, Agriculture
Health, Agriculture, Human Rights
Health, Human Rights
RANGPUR
NAOGAON
BOGRA
Rajshahi
NATORE
SIRAJGANJ
PABNA
KISHOREGANJ
Dhaka
RAJBARI
FARIDPUR
JESSORE
NARAIL
GOPALGANJ
CHANDPUR
LAKSHMIPUR
Khulna
Barisal
NOAKHALI
SATKHIRA
BAGERHAT
Chittagong
Bay of Bengal
COX'S BAZAR
Myanmar
N
W
E
S
1:2,800,000

2014 PROPOSED LGUS

ANNEX 2:

PROJECT EXTENSION YEAR 4 TASK AND TIMELINE

Bangladesh SDLG Project: Extension Year 4 Implementation Task and Timeline

	Q1 2014			Q2 2014			Q3 2014			Q3 2014			2015	
	Jan	Feb	Mar	Apr	May	Jun	Jul	Aug	Sep	Oct	Nov	Dec	Jan	Feb
Component 1: Roles and Authorities of Local Governments														
Task 1. National Conferences on LG Policy and Practice														
• National Conference on Upazila Policy and Practice					X	X								
• National Conference on 'Best Practices' in Local Service Delivery								X	X					
Component 2: Transparent and Effective Service Delivery by Local Governments														
• Foundational Activity 1: Organize Planning Meetings with Target LGUs and CIGs with Sector Participation		X	X	X	X	X	X							
• Foundational Activity 2: Establish Extension Period Technical Approach with Partner NGOs and USAID Sector Project Partners	X	X	X											
Task 1. Improve LGU Management Performance														
• Strengthen LGU Management Performance through Targeted Refresher Trainings				X	X	X	X							
• Demand-Driven Facilitation and Mentoring for LGUs						X	X	X	X	X	X			
• Peer Learning for New LGUs				X	X	X	X							
Task 2. Enhance LGU – Sector Collaboration for Service Delivery														
• Improve LGU Service Delivery through Trainings for Sector Standing Committees				X	X	X	X							
• Demand-Driven Facilitation and Mentoring for Standing Committees						X	X	X	X	X	X			
Component 3: Citizen Participation in Local Decision Making														
• Foundational Activity 1: Organize Planning Meeting with Target LGUs and CIGs with Sector Participation		X	X											
• Foundational Activity 2: Establish Extension Period Technical Approach with Partner NGOs	X	X	X											

	Q1 2014			Q2 2014			Q3 2014			Q3 2014			2015	
	Jan	Feb	Mar	Apr	May	Jun	Jul	Aug	Sep	Oct	Nov	Dec	Jan	Feb
Task 1. Improve Citizen Participation in Local Governance														
• Citizens-in-Governance Groups Refresher Training				X	X	X	X							
Task 2. Increase Citizen Oversight of LGUs and Sector Service Delivery														
• Community Drama with Focus on Standing Committees and Sector Issues				X	X	X	X	X	X	X	X			
• Citizen 'Eye Reporting' by Local Youth via Social Media					X		X	X	X	X	X			
Reporting and Performance Monitoring														
Annual Work Plans			X											
Quarterly Program Performance Reports			X	X			X			X			X	
Quarterly Financial Reports			X	X			X			X			X	
Success Stories (6 stories - intermittent)			X						X			X		
STTA Reports and Special Reports (intermittent)			X						X			X		

<u>**Key:**</u>

X = Activity Execution